On the WING

North American Birds 7

Andrea Voon
Richard Han

← 48-58 cm →

Belted Kingfisher

French: Martin-pêcheur d'Amérique

Little wings, little wings, flap flap flap...

Tunnel engineers in the lakes and ponds are on the wing.

Belted Kingfishers, Belted Kingfishers, clap clap clap...

Dig a secret burrow in full swing.

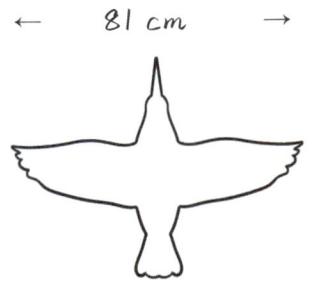

← 81 cm →

Black Oystercatcher

French: Huîtrier de Bachman

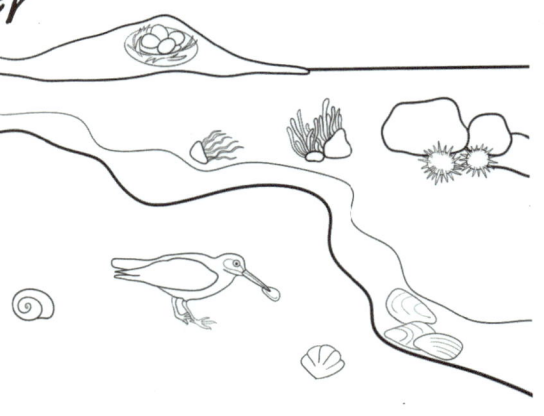

Great big wings, great big wings, flap flap flap...

Sword fighters along the shorelines are on the wing.

Black Oystercatchers, Black Oystercatchers, clap clap clap...

Jab and cut some shells in full swing.

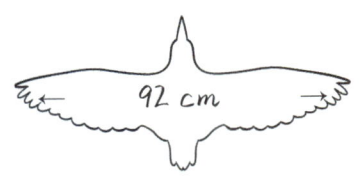

92 cm

American Bittern

French: Butor d'Amérique

Great big wings, great big wings, flap flap flap…

Living statues in the marshes are on the wing.

American Bitterns, American Bitterns, clap clap clap…

Stand still and stalk their prey in full swing.

Black-crowned Night Heron

French: Bihoreau gris

← 115 - 118 cm →

Great big wings, great big wings, flap flap flap...

Babysitters in the marshes are on the wing.

Black-crowned Night Herons, Black-crowned Night Herons, clap clap clap...

Brood any chick in their nest in full swing.

Ring-billed Gull

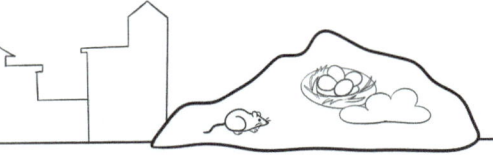

French: Goéland à bec cerclé

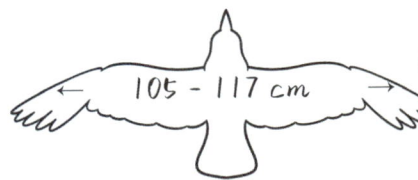

105 - 117 cm

Great big wings, great big wings, flap flap flap…

Jugglers on the lakes and ponds are on the wing.

Ring-billed Gulls, Ring-billed Gulls, clap clap clap…

Pluck and toss snack from the sky in full swing.

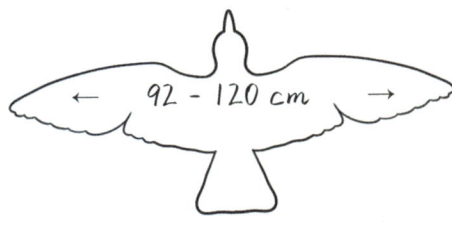

92 - 120 cm

Laughing Gull

French: *Mouette atricille*

Great big wings, great big wings, flap flap flap...

Summer tourists along the shorelines are on the wing.

Laughing Gulls, Laughing Gulls, clap clap clap...

Enjoy their island vacations in full swing.

California Gull

French: Goéland de Californie

130 cm

Great big wings, great big wings, flap flap flap...

Scavengers on the lakes and ponds are on the wing.

California Gulls, California Gulls clap clap clap...

Snap some alkali flies in full swing.

Great Egret

French: Grande Aigrette

131 - 145 cm

Great big wings, great big wings, flap flap flap...

Hatters in the marshes are on the wing.

Great Egrets, Great Egrets, clap clap clap...

Grow their long plumes in full swing.

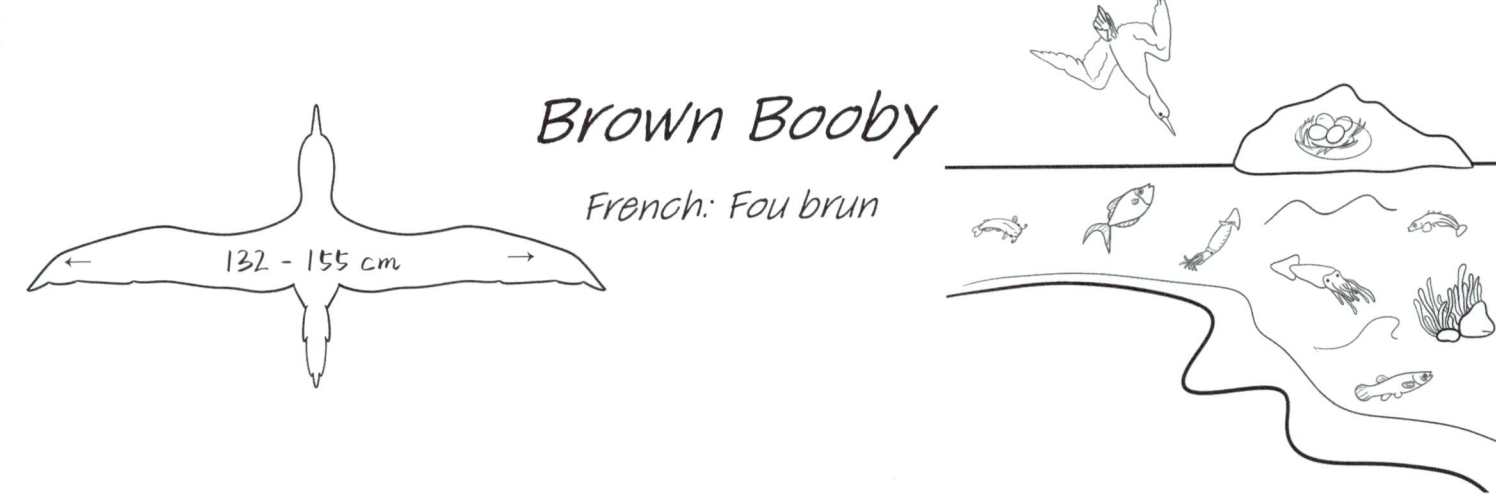

Brown Booby

French: Fou brun

132 - 155 cm

Great big wings, great big wings, flap flap flap...

Barbers in the oceans are on the wing.

Brown Boobies, Brown Boobies, clap clap clap...

Comb their feathers and spread some oils in full swing.

Masked Booby

French: Fou masqué

160 cm

Great big wings, great big wings, flap flap flap...

Arrow shooters in the oceans are on the wing.

Masked Boobies, Masked Boobies, clap clap clap...

Plunge-dive for fish and squid in full swing.

Brown Pelican

French: Pélican brun

← 200 cm →

Mighty wings, mighty wings, flap flap flap...

Marine forces in the oceans are on the wing.

Brown Pelicans, Brown Pelicans, clap clap clap...

Plunge-dive and scoop small fish in full swing.

American White Pelican

French: Pélican d'Amérique

244-290 cm

Humongous wings, humongous wings, flap flap flap…

Nurses on the lakes and ponds are on the wing.

American White Pelicans, American White Pelicans, clap clap clap…

Drive schooling fish toward shallow water in full swing.

Sanderling

Little wings, great big wings, flap flap flap…

Freshwater birds and seabirds are on the wing.

wading birds, diving birds, clap clap clap…

Hunt for aquatic animals in full swing.

whimbrel

Dunlin

Killdeer

Spotted Sandpiper

Ruddy Turnstone

Semipalmated Plover

Short-billed Dowitcher

Wilson's Snipe

Lesser Yellowlegs

Greater Yellowlegs

Author

Andrea Voon

Over the past few years, Andrea has learned and grown with her family as a full-time mother in Canada. Back in Malaysia, she was a Chinese immersion elementary school teacher. In 2021, Andrea started her journey as an author. Growing up in a multilingual environment, Andrea loves the beauty of languages on their own. She has the vision to publish picture books to support bilingual families in raising their children in English, Chinese, and Cantonese reading.

Photographer

Richard Han

Richard loves to practice patience through his lenses of the natural world. He enjoys observing the wildlife and photographing the natural lifestyles that animals live. He is excited to present the beautiful photos that he captured in dreamy tones and colors to all the birds lover.

BILINGUAL READING IS FUN!

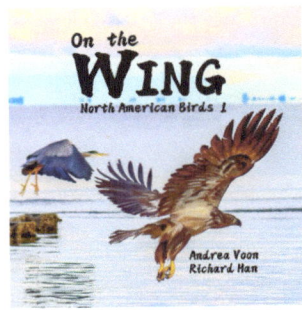
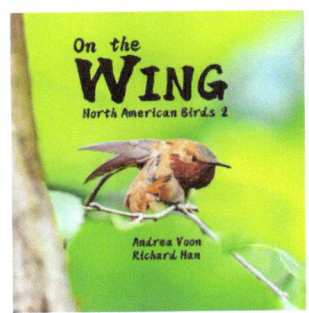
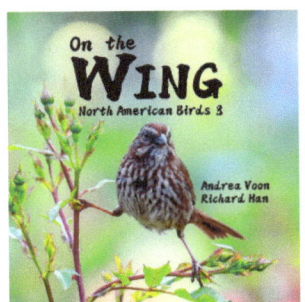
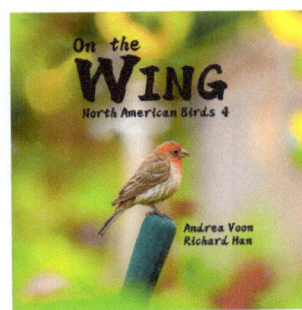

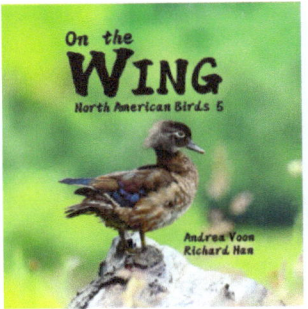

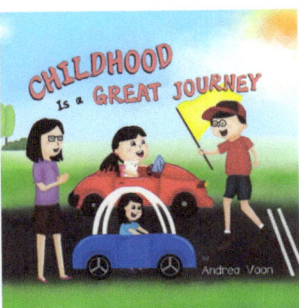

Check out other bilingual picture books by Andrea Voon.

To **Shirley Han, Derek, Eliana, Alayna & Magnus Dominus**

with love -- Andrea. V

For **Richard Han**
The patience in natural photography

ISBN 978-1-998856-59-6
Text copyright © 2025 Andrea Voon
Picture Credit © 2025 Richard Han

www.ingramcontent.com/pod-product-compliance
Lightning Source LLC
Chambersburg PA
CBHW041503120626
46547CB00003B/522